Meowditation

First published 2020 by Waverley Books, an imprint of
The Gresham Publishing Company Ltd, 31, Six Harmony Row,
Glasgow, G51 3BA, Scotland, UK

www.waverley-books.co.uk
info@waverley-books.co.uk
facebook/pages/waverleybooks

Text copyright © 2020 Eleanor Abraham
Illustrations copyright © 2020 Mark Mechan
Photographs, page 94 copyright © 2020 Eleanor Abraham

ISBN 978-1-84934-530-9

Printed and bound in the EU

Meowditation

A Cat's Guide
to Mindfulness and Pawsitivity

by Eleanor Abraham

WAVERLEY BOOKS

A Little About Me-ow

Hello. Are you sitting comfortably?
Not in my spot, I hope.

As you read, do you have a cat in your lap? If you're a cat's favourite seat, then you are blessed! You can't move now, but at least you have something lovely to read. It might be a while, so I hope you also have snacks, a nice cup of tea, your phone on silent, and your cordless pet vacuum and a lint roller by your side.

My name is Minnie. I live with My Human, and the Bearded One, and another cat, Max. It is a messy, happy, quite hairy house.

Some time ago, I lived in another house where there was a Nice Lady and lots of cats. I was very popular there for ages, but then one day this bossy cat arrived. She picked on me. I spent a lot of time hiding in the bathroom. The Nice Lady, probably wanting to shower alone again, thought the best thing was for me to be in charge of my own house.

And she was right. She phoned a friend she knew would be the right match for me, and I moved in with My Human and the Bearded One.

I had space to be myself again. Bliss!

And, boy, did my new housemates need my help. They liked my early morning alarm calls, housework supervision, cat hair distribution and head bumps. And I could purr them to sleep at night and make them laugh every day.

Celebrations! Or as we say in the cat world, fe-line-icitations.

Then Max arrived. He smelled weird. Worse than beard oil. It was hate at first sniff. He smelled like a boy – but it wasn't just that. This was *my* house! Every time we saw each other Max flopped, purred and flashed his (admittedly delightful) tum-tum, but I freaked. Whack! Hiss! Meowargh!

My Human and the Bearded One consulted something called a "cat behaviour book" with a picture of two happy, cuddly cat pals on the front – obviously actors.

They kept us separate till I felt more calm and Max started to smell better. These two things might be related. This took years. Well, not years, but from spider-hiding-time, till woo-hoo!-spider-snacks-time. It was the best of times (lots of liver paste treats and playing), it was the worst of times (invasion!) as some geezer once said about something unrelated.

But we all got a lot happier. Peace again. Now I'm still the boss and also an expert in calmness. After all that, My Human also needed a bit of calmness so I dictated this guide to her.

I advised her that being a bit more cat – or more lion – will improve your day and help you get some more balance. It can make you calmer if you need to be calm, or "zoomier" if you need a bit of zoom.

I hope my book will bring you some fun as well as some peace. Rather than staring at a boring candle or some wind chimes, I recommend a little bit of playing, nibble on some grass, climb up really high, run up the stairs, have a treat, chase a leaf, sniff something fascinating, and top it off with a lovely nap.

Happy meowditation!

Love Minnie.

Think Inside Your Box

All those self-help guides telling you to think outside of the box? Meh-eow. There's nothing nicer than getting into a lovely cardboard box to have a nice peaceful think.

Doesn't matter if it's a little small. Boxes are beautiful things and they must be sat in and appreciated.

The texture, the smell (what was in it before?), the dark, the lovely feeling of being enclosed on all sides. Irresistible.

When I'm in the box there's just me and the box; and my thoughts are about the box; also I might chew the box.

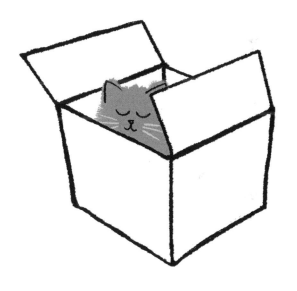

Routine

There is a universal order to everything in the world and this is it: wake up, run about a bit, eat, clean yourself, sleep.

I do this several times a day. I feel it is the responsibility of all cats, to encourage order and routine upon skittish, unpredictable humans.

I help the humans start the day, for example, by jumping from the wardrobe onto their bed or stomach to wake them up and then by shouting helpfully in their ear to alert them that it is time for my breakfast, in case they forgot. They rely on me for this invigorating welcome to the day.

Routine gives comfort and structure. When your routine is disrupted (such as, if a strange-smelling stranger comes to fix the boiler) following your other routines (such as, eating and then nervously washing your tummy) can soothe the nerves.

Cleaning

I maintain extreme focus when grooming. I do not wish to be petted when I am washing my tum-tum. I am a nice cat though. I will give you a little lick to remind you of how dirty and smelly and weird you are, daring to touch my nice clean fluffy tummy with your grubby hands that smell of hair gel or peanut butter. Colleagues of mine will bite you if you interrupt this most sacred of ceremonies and, while I abhor violence, I sympathise. Focus on the cleaning alone. No other thoughts are necessary. You may stop to chew upon a little tangly bit or a raggedy claw, but all the concentration of thought is on the bit you're cleaning, and then possibly the next bit you're cleaning, and then possibly "how on earth do I reach my bum since I put on weight?" No, no – cast all other thoughts away as soon as you experience them. Be pawsitive. You *will* reach your bum!

Staring

If I slow-blink while I stare at you it is my biggest compliment: I'm saying I love you. If I stare at you wide-eyed, with my pupils round and as black as your black, black heart; then watch out for your bare feet, I'm coming to get you.

Another type of stare involves deep concentration and spiders. I may have spotted that spider several hours ago, but regardless of whether it is still there lurking under the laundry basket, I am compelled to keep watch for that spider. The spider may now be the mere essence of a spider. A homeopathic dilution of the memory of a spider. I must keep watch over the spider absence, the negative spider, the antispider … until … snore. Wake me up at tea time.

Eating

In the wild, my relatives are hunting, eating small amounts as often as they can. A mouse liver here – a bird gizzard there. I prefer to eat this way too. In the home though, some of us may be faced with greedy companions, ready not only to wolf their own kittychunks, but to eat up yours too, in an unseemly gobbling session that invariably ends in #kittybarf.

Here's my solution. My humans have supplied me with an expensive, futuristic chip-operated food dish that only opens in my presence. I ignore this abomination. I demand food in a location away from Max, at a different hour, generally when he is asleep. I eat slowly and carefully, savouring every mouthful in a mindful and grateful way. Then he smells it, wakes up and steals it all anyway. I take some consolation in my sleek and elegant slimness compared to his podgy wobbly bot-bot.

Prey

I am sitting quietly. Like a loaf. Something scuttles. Things that scuttle are to be chased. And possibly eaten. I watch it, tensing the muscles of my back legs and wobbling my bottom in the approved manner. POUNCE! Whack. Poke. Whack again. Poke. Bite. I eat it! It tickles and is quite disgusting – more so even than the food the humans served up this week. My face contorts in a combination of disgust at the spider's taste and texture, but with the utter uncontained joy of having caught my own snack.

Even when I am resting I am alert. Aware of what is around me. Ready for disgusting and irresistible hairy arachnid snacks. It is possible to find joy even in such disgustingness.

Scratching

Little brown cardboard trays – the humans put them all over the place. As with most surfaces in existence, they are perfect for sleeping on. My preference is for a cardboardy surface rather than something soft and squishy that makes me lose my balance and overheat. These trays are intended to distract me from scratching the humans' worn-out old furniture. But who could get any pleasure from scratching that old rubbish? Waste of time. When they get a nice new couch I'll enjoy ripping that to shreds. Job satisfaction. But the cardboard things – they are very pleasing to scritch-scratch on. They feel nice on my paws and make a good noise when you scratch them. I close my eyes and imagine it is your lovely new leather couch. Scrippety-rip.

Sleepies

Sleepies are the best part of the day. They are a very big part of the day so most days are pretty good days if they involve plenty of sleepies. I like about 17 hours of sleepies depending on the weather, who is in the house, and what entertainment is available. They happen in various locations and various times. They follow a distinct pattern (see Routines). I am an expert sleeper and, through the employment of absolute stillness, concentration, and imagining I am a loaf of bread, I can go from intense bee chasing, to high quality napping in about 10 seconds, on any domestic surface. To achieve such high quality sleeps yourself, empty your mind of all bee-related thoughts and just be the bread. Buttered. I like butter.

Zoomies

Zoomies are the yang to the yin of sleepies. Because I'm such an award-winning sleeper, I have incredible energy and enthusiasm for athletics. Or maybe it's the other way round. Not sure. You already know the regimen I follow: intense exercise, snack, bit of a wash, five hours of sleep, repeat. In the absence of an adequate routine from the entertainment committee, I employ my own calisthenics. This takes place at the end of the day and may involve: running up the stairs, tearing back down the stairs, and hurtling around the top of the sofas. A quick respite is followed by the same again, and a sprint out the back door. Getting as high up as possible and shouting at the night sky is the perfect end to my routine. Snack time. Wash my face. Sleepies. The wheel of life turns once more.

Car Trips

I am a calm cat, usually. I like my routine. I sometimes mix it up a bit by sleeping on the window ledge or by the toilet pan, but normally I like the quiet life. One thing I despise is when I'm put in the cat box and off we go on a bloody car trip. It's noisy and hot and smelly, I hate Radio 4, and it makes me feel sick (the car, not Radio 4). It always ends with a visit to the vet rather than to somewhere nice like a cake shop. The vet is nice, and usually gives me a biscuit, but she also gave me an injection last time so I wasn't best pleased. Recently, my main human has taken to patting me and talking to me for the whole trip. She means well, but having a huge arm in my travel box is hardly fun. My preferred solution is to yowl the whole way. Like primal screaming – a nice way to let some stress out and also annoy the humans. Try it now!

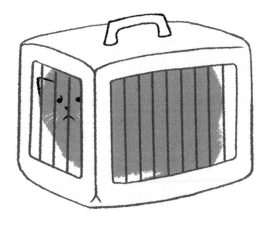

Treats

They say humans aren't trainable but I'm living proof that given the right trainer they are remarkably easy to influence. Repetition is the key. I am the master when it comes to getting treats. Let them think you're doing something for a reward when in fact your masterful manipulation is convincing them to repeatedly give you a treat in response to your behaviour.

You might say to me, "I think you've got that back to front." I don't care. I'm a positive thinker. It makes them happy to think I'm jumping on that special stool to get my treat. And it makes me happy to know that jumping on the stool will charm them into giving me a treat.

Win-win. Slurp.

Rain

I don't mind the rain, it's the wetness I don't like. The best way to enjoy the rain is from inside the house. Max is always hopeful that the rain won't be wet, and runs out excitedly. Then you hear a loud "broooop-priiiiip" which is his shorthand for "bloody hell it's wet out there after all", and he runs back in. Like it's a surprise.

"Rain is always wet," I tell him.

"I thought it would be OK this time," he says (or, actually, "prriiiiip-broooop").

Rain is wet. My companion is a bit daft. These things cannot be changed, and so we can only change the way we react to them.

Thus I content myself to stay in and enjoy the warmth and dryness of the nice warm couch when it rains, and I smile serenely and feel superior when Max runs out into a puddle again.

Instincts

I'm not entirely sure why, but I'm compelled to chew grass. My instincts are usually spot-on (like my immediate hatred for the boiler repair man) so, although it sounds weird (I was not, the last time I checked, a rabbit) I am sure it's the right thing to do.

In my catio there is a pot of grass, and every morning, before my exercises, I partake of a long pensive chew of it. I look very thoughtful and clever as I chew – which I am.

Eating it usually means that I will be sick soon afterwards, and I hate being sick, and I look less thoughtful and clever during a sick.

But I trust my instincts and, even though the sicky bit is unseemly, eating grass seems like the right thing to do. Max also feels the same, so I know it's not some weird craving that I get.

Anyway, we are none the worse for it, and maybe it even does us good to accept our natural instincts about our diet and listen to our bodies.

Sunbathing

Even in the coldest winters, if there's a tiny chink of sunshine available to me I will find it and enjoy it. Yes, I know … sunscreen; I'm not talking about outside though. A tiny chink of sunlight through the blind is enough to warm the tufts of the carpet and make it a lovely basking spot.

The warm patch moves. So, although I may be having a lovely sleep, I awaken, reposition myself and enjoy the heat again. The world never stands still, does it? We need to move with it and enjoy every bright spot when it reveals itself, especially in darker times.

My companion, as ever, there to burden me with his boorish ways, sometimes sneaks into the new spot of the moving sunbeam and beats me to it. Rude. But it has taught me not to be complacent or take things for granted

And there's always the window ledge.

Play

I'm not a kitten, but I love to play. Without play, I get mopey and grumpy and unfit. Cats who don't play are sad cats indeed.

Why don't humans play more? They are happier humans when they do. I see them working all the time, looking miserable and ignoring my requests to chase me. Me and Max are pretty good at making our own amusements (I tell him there are mice under the bed and that keeps him occupied for hours) but we have a better life when the entertainment committee put some thought into our activities. They'd have a better life too if they chased a ball of tinfoil round the room and worked a bit less.

Take the time every day to chase something shiny, colourful and slightly pointless – just for the pure fun of it.

Friends

I'm very comfortable in own company. However, I had a "friend" foisted upon me: Max. At first I was angry. He kept sleeping in my spots and eating my food. It has been difficult, but I have come to appreciate him ... or at least to notice him less. He is, usually, easygoing. I can be a bit tetchy. Max may be a nitwit but he has patience, a surprising gift for diplomacy, and is ... nice.

"Nice" – there are lots of better words, of course, but it works. Are you always nice? When you're angry, before you say anything, close your eyes and think of things that please and comfort you. Like spiders or butter.

Think how much worse getting angry makes things. Sure, you might get your way, and people might even smile the next time they see you, but they also might always remember that time you were horrible. Be more like my calm nitwit friend.

But don't try to eat a slug like he did.

Scary Things

In my youth there were many cats around me and also several dogs. I found some of the dogs quite scary but the worst that ever happened was that they gave me an unhygienic lick, or a sniff that invaded my privacy.

Sometimes things that seem scary and off-putting because of the way they look are actually fine. Of course sometimes things that are huge and scary are genuinely huge and scary. I get it.

What do I do when faced with such a thing?

1) Smack it. That doesn't necessarily always end well. 2) Hide. Depending on the level of peril, a sleep might be incorporated. 3) Pretend I don't care. I usually do this up quite high. And I can fit in a sleep too when I forget to be scared.

Scary things eventually go away. Mid-fright, it is worth remembering that.

Another thing you could do is imagine the thing you're scared of is exciting. Like spiders!

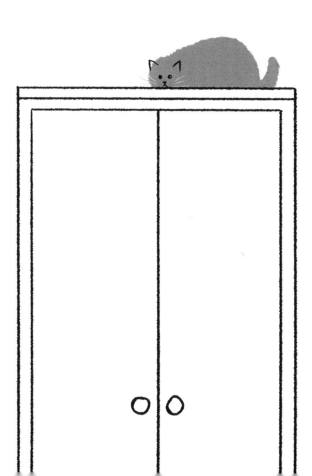

Climbing

There are lots of good things about climbing: the exercise, the view, when you get up high you can't be reached, and you can look down upon the masses (Max) with a feeling of achievement.

Also I get to stretch my claws and properly attack something. Looking down from up high, you feel all liony. And isn't it is great to get a different perspective on things?

Climbing up high gets me away from things that are bothering me. I feel very pleased with myself for being up high. Things look different up there.

How could you get a different angle on things?

You don't need to get on top of a wardrobe – though I do recommend it – you could just try to see the opposite view.

Squirrels

Tiny scuttling things are all very exciting; leaves are a beautiful thing to chase and behold; but one thing that usurps them all is … the squirrel! Its shuddery movements, its tempting twitchy tail, its speed! They're so fast you just can't catch them. Especially if you're in the house.

That doesn't stop Max and me – suddenly united in a common enemy – from watching the squirrel bounding along the garden fence. We watch from the window ledge or the catio, entertaining the vain hope that we can catch him. It's exhilarating even if it's unattainable.

Aspiring to things like a squirrel snack is a positive and hopeful thing to do. Even if the squirrel will never be ours it gives us a chance to forget our differences. (The main one being that I am very clever and Max is not.) We might be chasing some leaves, but you can be sure we're dreaming of squirrels.

Trees

I am an indoor cat – except for walks in my harness with the Bearded One, and my fresh-air breaks on the catio – but I do have experience of trees. One: they are the source of all the amazing leaves I see blowing about. Two: in an unsupervised moment, while Beardy was on the phone, I easily climbed a tree. It was great. Getting down was harder. Three: I have several structures the humans call cat trees. There are six in my house, which I feel is adequate. Real trees are best, but cat trees are excellent.

I spend a lot of time in life dodging people's feet, rubbing their ankles, or shouting at their knees. So it's good to be at a level where I can look the humans in the eye when I yell for my dinner, or give them a happy bunt in the forehead if the mood takes me.

Small humans climb trees, I wonder why big ones don't?

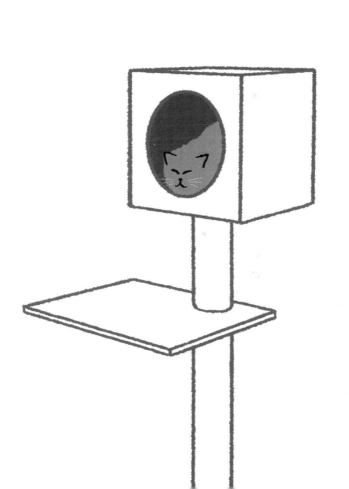

Change

I've heard it said that cats don't like change. Not strictly true. I do like my routines, but I like to change my routines now and again. Two weeks ago, my morning sleep was on the hammock in the cat tree. Last week the window ledge. This week it's on the couch.

This week I've been jumping on the table at dinner time which gets me a cuddle, which I don't mind if I know that food is coming soon. And last week I was drinking water out of the dripping tap in the bathroom sink instead of my bowl.

I like a bit of variety in my predictability.

If you're afraid of change that might be a good way to start. Something like having some water instead of coffee every morning. (Please. I don't like the smell.) Water is good.

Don't drink out of the toilet though.

Attention

I'm lying on your papers because I want your attention. That's it, really. I can't read. I'm not your office assistant. I don't want to help you with your accounts, though the paper has a nice feeling when I scratch it. I'm walking across your keyboard, not to write the next great postmodernist novel, but to get your attention. Mainly I need you to play with me. I'm not an ego maniac, I'm just stuck in the house all day and if you don't play with me I'll shred your balance sheet.

This is all a bit negative because you've neglected me a bit. We need to fit in play every day. You enjoy it too, don't pretend you don't. I'm curious to see what you're writing but I'd rather be running after that feather.

Take a break from work and play instead!

Paper

Despite what I said about not lying on your papers in order to help with your accounts, I do like paper in itself.

Paper is boring, you say. Paper is not squirrels. Or leaves.

Clearly – but paper is lovely. Tissue paper is my favourite and this is why: the texture, the lightness, the noise, the smell, it's lovely to jump on and then hide under; and skidding on it is also possible, which is fun. I saw on TV that it is made of trees. Crazy. Trees are amazing too.

Think about some everyday things that you don't appreciate enough that are actually amazing. Like me!

Memories

Long after something has gone, it can still remain fondly in the thoughts.

The mouse.

I maintain it is still in the kitchen though the humans don't want to believe it. Max found one outside and brought it in. It pretended to be dead and then made a run for it under the cooker. I sat there for days, it seemed, waiting for it to come out. I still think of it sometimes and then I return to stare, just in case it's been under there disguised as a chicken nugget all this time.

Lots of things will jog a memory, but sounds and smells can have a very powerful effect.

Certain smells that I make certainly get the humans' attention.

Birds

When I'm inside (on the window ledge usually) and I see a bird outside that I want to eat (and I've yet to meet one that didn't look tasty) I involuntarily make a sound that I've been told sounds like birds chirping. It's like a cross between a meow and teeth chattering.

What am I saying to those delicious birds? I can't tell you, but if you were broadcasting it you'd probably have to beep it out.

My favourite toys involve feathers – I've been training with them all my life to ensure I would have a successful bird hunt should I get the chance.

The best feather is one you find randomly on the ground. It still smells of a bird. The humans will take it off me if they see it in case of bird germs. Bah. I'm made of stronger stuff!

Full disclosure: I have not ever caught and killed a bird, but I have eaten chicken.

Moths

Just before bedtime (human bedtime, that is – I have several bedtimes), I often get a burst of energy. The universe answers this need by the existence of what I like to call "the flying cat-biscuit": the moth. On summer nights they sneak into the house via open windows, and settle themselves near lamps and lights that they have mistaken for the moon. When these lights are extinguished, the moths mistake my human's face for the moon, fluttering into her eye, and making her squeal and run.

They are a challenge to catch if they are up high, but if they flutter too low I get a nice easy night-time snack. Crunchy with a soft centre.

I then check on the human, who has gone to bed, fearful of the next moth collision. I breathe on her face with my moth breath, tickling with my whiskers, and she squeals again.

Moths are fun!

Haters

It's quite easy to spot humans who don't like me. They bristle when they see me. They think I'm scary or dangerous. Nonsense – though I am a threat to spiders, it's true.

They say cats look aloof and superior. Moi? Well I am superior, I can't help that, but I'm not usually aloof, especially if you've got treats.

I'm not worried about these people. I'll approach them anyway, safe in the knowledge that they won't try to pick me up or kiss or cuddle me. This makes me so happy that ironically I want to show them some affection. Which they hate. Oops!

Someone acts like you coated their corduroys in cat hair? It's not worth wondering why they don't like you – that's their problem. Instead think of the clever people who are not jealous of your fluffiness, and who recognise your genius!

Strangers

When visitors come to the house I usually enjoy meeting them, sniffing them, and sitting next to them to see how much cat hair will stick to them before they notice.

However … painters, plumbers, boiler-repair people, builders … No offense, but you upset me. You thump through my house, sawing or hammering things, or playing radio stations I don't like. Smelling of turps and stuff that could poison me. The humans put me in a cage or a room so I don't run away if you leave the doors open.

My only recourse in the face of this chaos is to shut my eyes and meditate. I'm not really sleeping here. I'm not even really thinking. I close my eyes and let my thoughts disappear like spiders running for cover when you move a plant pot.

This allows the time to pass as calmly as possible, in a way that anxiously scraping the carpet up and wedging it behind the door didn't.

The Power of Meow

When me and Max are alone we do not make a lot of noise. We communicate in sniffs, licks, blinks and hard stares; and occasionally I will whack him, but in a loving way for his own good.

The only people I speak to with my voice are the humans. They speak gibberish back to me but it almost feels like a real conversation sometimes, bless them.

Max only talks to them at meal times with his usual "briiiip" which means "hurry up, I'm hungry".

My meows can mean lots of things: I want to go out, I want to play, clean out my litter tray, food please, treats please, scritches please, can we go for a walk, shift over I want to sit where you're sitting. They usually assume it's food I'm after – which is incorrect, but not the worst assumption. It's usually play that I want. They eventually work that out ... after several treats.

Fur

Squeak, squeak, squeak. Squeak, squeak. Squeak, squeak, squeak, squeak. Squeak, squeak.

No not a mouse – but the plaintive squealing of a plastic lint roller in action, (partially) removing fluffy white cat hairs from human clothes.

Sometimes I find My Human gently weeping, as she misses bus after bus trying to remove all my beautiful hairs from black jersey material. I'm covered in them and they look gorgeous on me. What's the problem?

It's all about how you see things, isn't it? If you're covered in cat hairs it means a cat loved you enough to share your chair, bed, laundry basket, ironing board, or even that they reluctantly allowed you to give them a big cuddle.

Next time you get sad because your good interview suit is covered in fur, remember it means that you share your house with a gorgeous fluffy creature that loves you.

Also you need to vacuum more.

Focus

I wait patiently. Relaxed but focussed. I'm beneath the dinner table. This is a good spot in itself, but I aspire to more. Occasionally, little pieces of sausage drop from above, but that is just a fortunate perk rather than my main purpose.

Chair legs scrape back. I must move quickly. The Bearded One is on his usual quest for ketchup and it is my turn to move in our daily game of strategy. He rises from his seat to go to the cupboard, and before he has even got there I'm already in his seat and My Human is laughing.

My favourite seat is mine once more. Well, one of them. Thanks to concentration, speed and persistence – and ketchup.

Scratching an Itch

My companion does this very amusing thing with his face when he has an itch to scratch. He sticks his chin out and sort of chews at a nonexistent thing while he scritchy-scratches his neck with his back leg.

Well, I found it very amusing up until he pointed out I do exactly the same thing. He's right. I saw myself reflected in the china cabinet. I'm even worse than him.

Now I know why the humans call to each other whenever I scratch my neck. "Come and see her! She's doing the chin thing!"

Scratching an itch is one of life's under-appreciated things. As long as it's not due to fleas or a rash or chicken pox or something, so what if I make a funny face.

The Window Ledge

The window ledge – any window ledge – is a prime location. It's a safe, warm place to view nasty-rainy-snowy-windiness. And on a frosty sunny day, lying sprawled in a ray of sunlight, I can almost believe it's still summer.

I chirrup to the fat pigeons I spy on the lawn, informing them, from a comfortable distance, of how very delicious they look. They're safe. It's too nice here to move, and there's also that inconvenient pane of glass between us. It feels private behind the curtain but apparently I am visible because various humans wave to me. I watch next door's dog peeing on our hedge and a blackbird with a worm in its beak land in a tree. It's all go.

It's sad that humans are too big to sit on the window ledge, but then, you have TV.

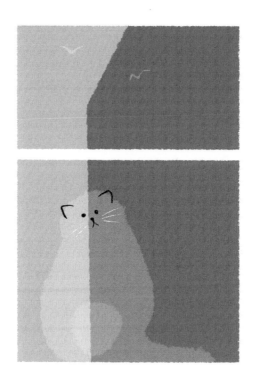

In the Moment

Shoved in the cat box with no warning. Then the awful car trip. Then an injection, or getting my bits squeezed, or poking at my teeth and gums, or getting my temperature taken. Highly unseemly! Then another car trip. Too much!

The vet – it's very upsetting at the time. Afterwards, I might stay quiet for quite a long time but I always eventually feel better.

This is the best thing about bad stuff that has happened: it is no longer happening.

Other stuff happens, and if that is good then I feel good.

That is the way of cats. We live in the moment. If we have contented fulfilled present lives, we don't spend time dwelling on the past.

Also, humans, you're only as good as your last treat, remember that.

Catstrovert

Am I an introvert or an extrovert? Me, I hate labels. Aren't we all a bit of a mixture? Sometimes I feel curious and confident and sociable, and I might bunt you on the head or want to play. And sometimes I'll sleep behind the couch till I want to come out and be very grumpy if I'm disturbed. Often I want to be quiet but I still want some company while I do that, so I'll watch you typing or doing the dishes while I silently supervise.

Max seems more sociable than I am because of his permanent goofy, friendly expression, but I'm the one who will sit next to you and blink at you if you've gone to bed feeling unwell. (The fact that your fever makes you deliciously cosy and warm is just a coincidence.)

If you aren't easily defined as introvert or extrovert why not say you're a catstrovert – someone who likes talking and being quiet and playing and sleeping and resting and activity?

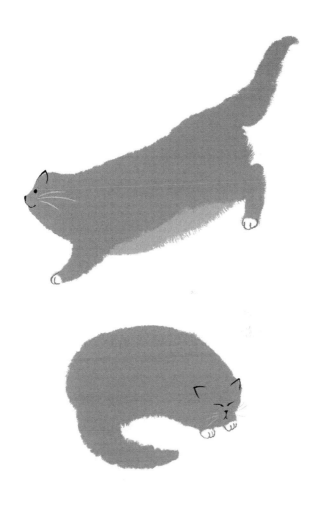

Walking Away

In my last house I was getting picked on. Hard to believe, given my confidence and management skills now, but I was.

Whatever I did, this other cat would hit me or make sure I was excluded from the group. I had to walk away. First of all, I hid in the bathroom. Soon after, though, I moved to my new home. I fitted in right away, and soon became the boss.

The thing about bullies is, it's not you it's them; so changing what you do isn't the solution. Whatever you do will never be good enough for them. And you can't make anyone else change unless they want to. So probably the best thing you can do is get away from them.

For a while I almost became a bully. I resented Max when he arrived, and I was mean. But that was all about me feeling unhappy. My family worked very hard to make me feel secure and I was soon adorable and nice again.

Comfort Zones

It's not that I don't like comfort, it's just that my idea of comfort includes a lot more options than yours. I don't mind a hard surface – often I prefer it. Tables, chairs, cushions, grass, wood, keyboards, blankets – my perfect combination is a cosy blanket on a hard surface up quite high. I like your bed too. The bit in the very middle is the best bit so that you have to hang off the side. It's a good exercise for your core. (Not really. I've no idea. I'm not a personal trainer, you know, I'm a cat.)

The humans got me a squishy, round doughnut bed. It was wonderfully soft, made of nice material and was a lovely size. Awful. All comfy and cosy. So wrong.

The seemingly obvious comfy option isn't necessarily so for everyone. We're all different, with different comfort zones.

I did like the bag the bed came in though.

One Thing

Cats do not multi-task. Cats do one thing at a time and focus on that. That's why we are such high achievers.

I regularly see humans trying to do two, or even three, things at once.

For example, the Bearded One reads Twitter off his phone while we go out for a walk. This enables me to run up trees or into the neighbours' long grass when he is not looking.

My Human tries to type and make dinner and play with me and listen to podcasts at the same time. She does them all very badly as a result. This makes her grumpy, and as unpleasant as the dinner. She should just play with me!

When I do one thing – like washing myself, staring at a spot in the distance, or hunting a spider – I give it my entire concentration. It makes the job more enjoyable, and successful.

Alone Time

I'm not talking about feeling lonely. That is entirely another thing and can happen in a room that's full of other cats. I'm talking about enjoying your own company. Enjoying being able to be a little bit selfish – in a good way – and making all your own decisions. Having some lovely time to yourself without having to ask someone else if it's OK or compromising. I compromise all the time. Like, I allow Max to sometimes eat first, or sleep up at the top of the best cat tree, or sit in the sunny spot. And we spend a lot of time together on our catio sharing the best lookouts, watching for hedgehogs and squirrels and frogs. That's nice of course. But when he is asleep, and no one else is in, I sometimes just run up and down the stairs for the pure fun of it, or stretch out on the window ledge and sleep behind the curtain. Bliss!

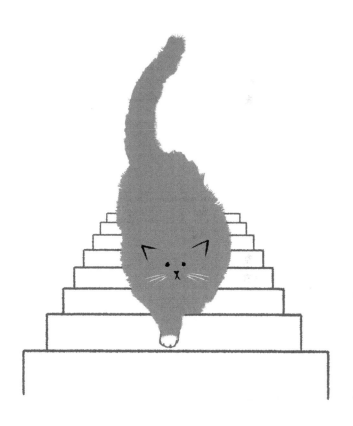

Your Bag

Bags are the best thing ever. Even better than boxes, and boxes are pretty good. That's where the saying comes from – "That's my bag." It means the thing that is "your bag" is the very best possible thing ever, ever. (I think.)

Bags are my bag. Big brown paper bags are superb, but big rustly plastic bags are also excellent.

Getting in the bag or on the bag is best. Humans carry stuff in bags, which I feel is a wasted opportunity. They are an excellent place on which to sleep or shelter from the hot sun; a place to rest, think, play, scratch and excavate. Playing with a toy while rolling on a big rustly paper or plastic bag is a joy. When I am in a bag I often forget there are other people around – and while me and Max were still not getting along, bags helped me feel calm.

Find your bag – something calming, or fun or playful – every day.

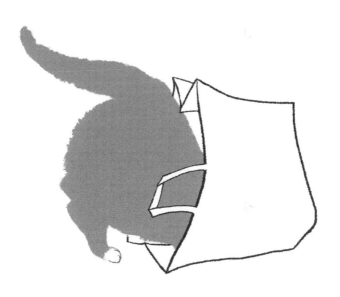

Be More Lion

I am only little, but I have a very big personality. I have a loud voice too, when I choose to use it. You can do this too. Speak up for yourself.

Tell people what you want. You can get liver treats if you ask for them, I have found. You might find that they didn't know you wanted liver treats.

Do you want liver treats? Or something else? (I can't now think of anything I want more than liver treats so it's hard to say what you might want.)

Be bold. Would a lion wait patiently for her dinner to trip over and invite itself into her tummy? No – she'd go and catch it! If you want something go out and grab it!

The Tummy

Another thing upon which me and my housemate disagree: he is all about the tummy tickles, but I will take deep offense should you invade my tumty space. And while I am far too nice to bite anyone, you will have to live with my disdain, which is far more cutting.

Speaking for my friend, he really does love his belly rubbed, for some reason. He'll go into a weird smiley trance for as long as the human is willing to massage his fat tum-tum. Perhaps it is related to his own gluttony. Maybe he is overdeveloped in that area somehow? Whatever the reason, I can take pleasure in his happiness for a couple of reasons: his weird goofy face is highly amusing, and I'm very much relieved it's not me.

Help

I'm very independent so I don't take kindly to interference with my grooming. But, I have a lush and thick coat and my tiny dainty mouth can't quite cope with it sometimes. I have to accept help. Brushing.

Max has less of a problem in this area, having a tongue that could strip paint off a door. He sometimes gets distracted and ends up grooming the carpet and doesn't notice.

I think it is hard to accept help because we maybe feel less independent for asking for it. It maybe feels like a weakness. But when others care about us they want to help us. It feels good to help others; so do a good deed and let someone help you when you need it.

Epilogue

I always thought we'd have to wait till we retired till we got pets. That would have been sensible, but I'm glad we didn't. In October 2017 Saorsa came to live with me and Bill. She was a delight – good natured, full of personality and cheekiness – and we quickly became besotted and the ultimate cat bores.

I blame Bill, but after a year of being cat owners we (Bill) thought maybe Saorsa needed a friend, in case she got lonely. My cousin Marion Collins – Saorsa's previous owner – had the very cat. One of Saorsa's own children: Georgette (Georgie). Mother and daughter – they were bound to get on! Oh dear.

Saorsa was very unhappy and anxious and quite angry. She stopped playing, she stopped eating (except for liver treats) and she did *not* want to be pals with Georgie. Four months on, a carpet ruined by a hundredweight of liver paste, consultations with a cat behaviourist (thank you, Kim Houston), scores of YouTube videos (thank you, Jackson Galaxy), several books, and internet forum questions, and they finally could be in a room together unsupervised, calmly ignoring each other. My dream of them being the best of cat pals was still far off, but at least they could share the house.

It took a year. Almost exactly a year after their reintroduction they seemed to finally like each other. I didn't think it would ever happen.

They now play together, plot mice and frog captures, watch for squirrels and hedgehogs, greet each other by touching noses, and sleep quite near each other (though not snuggled up like some of the internet cats).

People face much bigger problems in life but for about six months this took over our lives. Things are much calmer now, thank goodness.

Saorsa is back to being gentle and funny and has resumed bumping Bill on the beard. And Georgie, who tolerated so much in the time it took Saorsa to calm down, is an adorable goofball who loves playing as much as she loves eating.

The pair of them make us laugh even on the grumpiest days.